First World War
and Army of Occupation
War Diary
France, Belgium and Germany

51 DIVISION
Divisional Troops
232 Machine Gun Company
13 July 1917 - 28 February 1918

WO95/2857/3

The Naval & Military Press Ltd
www.nmarchive.com
Published in association with The National Archives

Published by

The Naval & Military Press Ltd

Unit 10 Ridgewood Industrial Park,

Uckfield, East Sussex,

TN22 5QE England

Tel: +44 (0) 1825 749494

www.naval-military-press.com

www.nmarchive.com

This diary has been reprinted in facsimile from the original. Any imperfections are inevitably reproduced and the quality may fall short of modern type and cartographic standards.

© **Crown Copyright**
Images reproduced by permission of The National Archives, London, England, 2015.

Contents

Document type	Place/Title	Date From	Date To
Heading	WO95/2857-3		
Heading	51st Division 232nd Machine Gun Coy Jly 1917-1918 Feb		
Miscellaneous	On His Majesty's Service.		
Heading	War Diary For 232nd Co Machine Gun Corps (51st) Highland Division From 1st To 31st July 1917		
War Diary	Havre	13/07/1917	19/07/1917
War Diary	In The Field	20/07/1917	24/07/1917
War Diary	St Julian Sector	25/07/1917	04/08/1917
War Diary	In The Field	06/08/1917	06/08/1917
War Diary	St Julien Sector	07/08/1917	03/09/1917
War Diary	Map Reference Poelcapelle 1/10000 Edition 2	06/09/1917	23/09/1917
War Diary	Map Reference Belgium Sheet 28	24/09/1917	26/09/1917
War Diary	Map Reference Hazebrouck 59 & Lens.11	30/09/1917	01/10/1917
Heading	War Diary Of 232nd Co Machine Gun Corps From 1st To 31st October 1917		
War Diary	Map Reference 51 B M.16.b.90.40	04/10/1917	04/10/1917
War Diary	Map Reference France 51B. S.W	04/10/1917	31/10/1917
War Diary	Map Reference France 51B. S.W.	17/10/1917	26/10/1917
Heading	War Diary Of 232nd Co M.G Corps From 1st To 30th November 1917 Vol 5		
War Diary	Map Ref. Lens. 11 Edition 2 1/100.000.	01/11/1917	14/11/1917
War Diary	France 57c SE	15/11/1917	19/11/1917
War Diary	Map Reference France 57c S.E.	20/11/1917	20/11/1917
War Diary	Marcoing 57C NE	21/11/1917	23/11/1917
War Diary	Map Reference	24/11/1917	25/11/1917
War Diary	Lens 11.	26/11/1917	30/11/1917
Heading	War Diary 232nd Co. M.G. Corps From 1st To 31st December 1917 Vol 6		
War Diary	Map Reference	01/12/1917	01/12/1917
War Diary	Lens. 11.	02/12/1917	02/12/1917
War Diary	France 57 C N.E.	02/12/1917	25/12/1917
War Diary	Demicourt K7c 9.4.	26/12/1917	28/12/1917
War Diary	Demicourt K2 B 90.95	29/12/1917	31/12/1917
Heading	War Diary Of 232nd Co. M.G. Corps. From 1st To 31st Jan 1918 Vol 7		
War Diary	Demicourt K7c 9.4 and 57c. N.E. France	01/01/1918	31/01/1918
Heading	War Diary Of 232nd Co. M.G. Corps From 1st To 28th February 1918 Vol 8		
War Diary	Map. Courcelles 1/10000	01/02/1918	09/02/1918
War Diary	France 57c N.W.	10/02/1918	10/02/1918
War Diary	France Part Of 57C	10/02/1918	10/02/1918
War Diary	France 57c N.W.	11/02/1918	12/02/1918
War Diary	Map. France Part Of 57C	13/02/1918	19/02/1918
War Diary	France Part Of 57C	20/02/1918	28/02/1918

WO95/28857/3

51ST DIVISION

232ND MACHINE GUN COY.
JLY 1917-MAR ~~1919~~
1918 FEB

Vol 2

ON HIS MAJESTY'S SERVICE.

232 M.G. Company.

War Diary.

B

This file is only issued as a cover to Army Form C 2118 (War Diary).

Vol. I

Confidential

War Diary

for

232nd Co. Machine Gun Corps.
(51st (Highland) Division)

from 1st to 31st July, 1917.

SHEET ONE

Army Form C. 2118.

232 M.G. Coy
(51ST HIGHLAND DIVISIONAL M.G. COY)

WAR DIARY
or
INTELLIGENCE SUMMARY.
(Erase heading not required.)

Instructions regarding War Diaries and Intelligence Summaries are contained in F.S. Regs., Part II. and the Staff Manual respectively. Title pages will be prepared in manuscript.

Place	Date	Hour	Summary of Events and Information	Remarks and references to Appendices
HAVRE	13.7.17		The 232ND M.G. Coy landed at HAVRE from ENGLAND, - 5 Officers and 100 O.R. on S.S. "ANTRIM", 5 Officers, 77 O.R. and Transport on S.S. "HULLSET". Encamped at No. 1. 20 Camp.	
do	19.7.17	11.20 A.M.	The 232ND M.G. Coy marched from No. 1. Camp and entrained at Point 4 GARE DE MERCHANDISE. Train started at 4 P.M. The following officers landed and are enroute with the Company: Capt. D.N. WIMBERLEY (Q.O. CAMERON HRS) C.O.; Lt. A.J. STEWART. (P.W.O. WEST YORKSHIRE REGT.) 2ND I/C; Lt. C.H. HASTINGS, M.G.C., Lt. A.S. PULLEY, (1ST CO. LONDON REGT); Lt. F.C.T. WOODHEAD (5TH WORCESTERS); Lt. B WEBB (3 N. STAFFS REGT) 2ND Lt. A.F. HOLMES (M.G.C); 2ND Lt. R.L. HENDERSON (M.G.C); 2ND Lt. G BROADBENT (M.G.C) and 2ND Lt. R.E. SAYNOR (M.G.C)	
IN THE FIELD	20.7.17	3 PM	Detrained at POPERINGHE and marched to "D" Camp (MARFEE BELGIUM Sheet 28 N.W. A 30.C) and taken on strength of 51ST HIGHLAND DIVISION as DIVISIONAL M.G. Coy.	
	21.7.17	8.30	C.O. and 4 Officers reconnoitred the trenches in the ST JULIAN SECTOR. The enemy dropped some shrapnel over the wood in which we are billetted. No Casualties.	
	22.7.17		Half teams from all sections moved off at intervals from 5.30 PM to relieve guns of 32ND and 154TH M.G. Coys in the ST JULIAN SECTOR, remainder of Coy. remaining in Camp at "9.30" Central. Advanced Coy H.Q. moving to Dug-outs on the W. Bank of YSER CANAL. "B" and "D" Sections under Lt. WEBB and 2ND Lt. HOLMES to SUPPORT LINES and R.S.C. doing harassing fire from the rear in neighbourhood of BURNT FARM.	
	23.7.17		Operations nil. One gun and one and one third of "D" Section out of action. No casualties. Harassing guns fired 12,000 rounds indirect at positions in rear of enemy lines.	
	24.7.17		Harassing guns fired 15,000 rounds on points in rear of BOESL LINES. 1 O.R. gassed. Took over the front from 39TH DIVISION	
ST JULIAN SECTOR	25.7.17		One gun each of "B" and "D" Sections joined in artillery barrage for daylight raids carried out by 9TH SHERWOOD FORESTERS and 1/7. ARGYLL & SUTHERLAND HRS. / "D" Section particularly got good targets and caught a party of the enemy retiring across the open near CANADIAN FARM firing three belts at them and inflicting heavy casualties. The Coy was afterwards congratulated personally by BRIG GEN DALY G.O.C. 33RD BDE and also received messages from the ARMY CORPS and DIVISIONAL COMMANDERS. 228 M.G. Coy relieved five of our guns, teams returning to Billets at TRANSPORT LINES.	
do	26.7.17		Harassing guns fired 16,000 rounds on areas in rear of enemy lines. The two guns at HIGHLAND and FUSILIER FARMS were both subjected to intermittent shelling throughout the day. No casualties.	
	27.7.17	30 P.M.	During the evening word was received that the enemy had retired from his forward positions, and patrols of the K.S. STAFFS were sent out to reconnoitre. The Coy. was ordered to send a Section over our FARM as the Infantry had consolidated. "B" Section under 2ND Lt. HENDERSON was moved up this purpose to FOCH FARM and that told to await orders.	

SHEET TWO

232 M G Coy   Army Form C. 2118.

WAR DIARY
or
INTELLIGENCE SUMMARY.
(57ST DIVISIONAL M.G. Coy.)
(Erase heading not required.)

Instructions regarding War Diaries and Intelligence Summaries are contained in F. S. Regs., Part II. and the Staff Manual respectively. Title pages will be prepared in manuscript.

Place	Date	Hour	Summary of Events and Information	Remarks and references to Appendices
	27.7.17	11.30 pm	The order to advance cancelled. "A" Section moved off from FOCH FARM about 12.15 a.m.-12.30 a.m. 27.25th for harassing fire. "D" Section. (Lt. A.F. HOLMES) meanwhile had been sent for from transport lines and arrived about this time.	
	28.7.17	3.30 am	"A" Section and one team of "C" Section moved from harassing to barrage positions to join in CHINESE attack. The guns opened at 3.50 a.m. and continued until 5.49 am firing 7,000 rounds and getting no retaliation.	
ST. JULIAN SECTOR.	29.7.17		The harassing guns fired 16,250 rounds on areas in rear of enemy's lines during the night 28-29th	
"	30.7.17		The harassing guns fired 18,500 rounds on areas in rear of enemy's lines during the night 29-30 th.	
"			The 3 defensive guns (one of D and 2 of B) in the line withdrew during the night 30-31 to the CANAL BANK the assaulting guns of the Division having moved into their assembly area. The harassing fire guns fired no rounds during the night, unharassing about 2 hours before Zero.	
"	31.7.17		The Division attacked at 3.50 a.m. 232 M G Coy being in reserve at Canal Bank. Objectives reached and consolidated. About noon orders were received that eight guns were to proceed immediately and take over "B" barrage positions in captured front line system from 23. M.G. Coy. "B" and "D" Sections were accordingly sent up, Lt. WEBB in Command. At 4 p.m. orders to withdraw four guns were received and word was sent for "B" Section to return. "D" Section moved slightly forward in front of KEMPTON PARK and consolidated, the Officer i/c deciding that as he had a field of fire of over 15,000 yards and covered the STEENBECK RIVER from the L.O.A. going up Kaza guns were in no better not to move further forward that night. About 2.30 p.m. on the L.O.A. going up Kaza guns went on the barrage laid down.	28 N.W. 1/10,000
"	1.8.17		"B" Section went forward to relieve 152. M.G.Coy. guns in position around the block line with Section H.Q. at GATEWICK. Map of ST JULIAN. This was accomplished without casualties. These guns are defensive and are laid on L.O.S. lines covering the LANGEMARK ZONNE BECK ROAD and also protecting the Division right flank. Position of guns around 15 G 80.90	28 N.W. 1/10,000
"	4.8.17		The four guns in position around FORT (CALEDONIA) moved forward to BRITANNIA FARM and consolidated	

Army Form C. 2118.

WAR DIARY
or
INTELLIGENCE SUMMARY.
(Erase heading not required.)

Instructions regarding War Diaries and Intelligence Summaries are contained in F. S. Regs., Part II. and the Staff Manual respectively. Title pages will be prepared in manuscript.

No. 21 A
HIGHLAND DIVISION

Place	Date	Hour	Summary of Events and Information	Remarks and references to Appendices
In the field St Jansten Biezen	6/8/17		Rear detachment moved to A.30 central point.	
	7.8.17		Relief of the Company by 32 Tn. Coy commenced. Four guns near VON WERDER HOUSE and MACDONALDS WOOD being relieved.	
	8.8.17		Remaining two guns in front line relieved. French party entrained at VLAMERTINGHE at St JANSTEN BIEZEN. Remainder of Company marched from A.30 central to TUNNELLING Camp, St JANSTEN BIEZEN. Map reference Belgium + France Sheet 27.	
	9.8.17		Refitting Company.	
	10.8.17		Map reference HAZEBROUCK 5A 1/100,000. The Company with 152 Infantry Brigade moved back by rail to EPERLECQUES AREA. The H.Q and four guns detraining at PROVEN at 8 a.m. detaining at WATTEN with orders to billet at WEST ROYE AFCHEMONT found out that billets had been changed to ESTMONT. Transport moved by road initiating for the night at WORMHOUDT.	
	11.8.17		Training and refitting. Transport arrived at ESTMONT during the afternoon. Relief was notified by Major General G.M HARPER, C.B., D.S.O, G.O.C 51st Highland Division.	
	15.8.17		Map reference HAZEBROUCK 5A 1/100,000. Transport moved from EPERLECQUES area to St JANSTER BIEZEN by road reaching for the night at WORMHOUDT.	
	22.8.17		Map reference HAZEBROUCK 5A 1/100,000. (1) 232 MG Company (reserved only) moved by road from EPERLECQUES area to TUNNELLING Camp, St JANSTER BIEZEN entraining at WATTEN on the evening of the 23rd and detraining at ABEELE about midnight.	
	23.8.17		(2) The transport completed their march arriving at TUNNELLING Camp at 2.30 p.m.	
	24.8.17		The Company marched from ABEELE to Tunnelling Camp, arriving about 4.30 p.m.	
	25.8.17		TUNNELLING CAMP	

WAR DIARY
or
INTELLIGENCE SUMMARY.
(Erase heading not required.)

Army Form C. 2118.

Place	Date	Hour	Summary of Events and Information	Remarks and references to Appendices
St Jean-ter-Biezen	29/8/17		Map Ref. Sheets 27 and 28 1/40,000. Brigadier 154 Bde Group (154 Infantry Bde and 232nd M.G. Coy.) moved from TUNNELLING CAMP, ST JANSTER BIEZEN to MURAT CAMP with transport at HOSPITAL FARM, 232 M.G. Coy leaving starting point (Road Junction L4672) at 5.30 a.m., and reaching their destination about 9.30 a.m. and finished camp.	
	30/8/17		Map Reference POL E CAPPELLE Ed.1 1/10000. 232 Divisional M.G. Coy received orders to attack a section of four guns to the 152 Bde M.G. Coy on the night 30/31. These guns to be moved on West side of STEENBEEK and take up positions on the line RED FARM - FERDINAND FARM, COMEDY FARM for the defence of the STEENBEEK.	
	31/8/17		C/Section under Lt WOODHEAD moved into position on line ordered on the morning 31/8/17.	
	1/9/17		Map Reference POLECAPPELLE Ed.1 1/10000. Orders received from C/Section in position West of RIVER STEENBEEK to carry out road and night firing on certain points in rear of enemy's lines.	
	2/9/17		Four teams of A Section relieved C/Section W. of RIVER STEENBEEK relieving being complete at 2.15 a.m.	

D. Dunlesley Capt
Commanding
232 M.G. Coy.

WAR DIARY
— or —
INTELLIGENCE SUMMARY.
(Erase heading not required.)

Army Form C. 2118.

Place	Date 1917	Hour	Summary of Events and Information	Remarks and references to Appendices
POELCAPPELLE Map reference 1/10,000 Edn. 2	Sept 6th		The 4 teams of "A" section were relieved by "D" section on the morning of the 6th. A daylight raid was carried by the Infantry, a slow barrage being put up by the 4 guns at FERDINAND FARM. 4000 rounds fired on enemy roads etc.	
	Sept 7th		Orders received from Division to place 2 teams in HAANIXBEEK FARM. The guns to be escorted by one platoon of Infantry.	
	Sept 8th		2 teams of "B" section placed in HAANIXBEEK FARM. Night firing on enemy lines fired on during the night, 3000 rounds being expended. Points in rear of enemy roads and tracks. HAANIXBEEK is under direct observation, and can therefore only be reached at night or in a dawn mist. By day the teams are confined to the dug-out, only coming out to man their guns in case of an attack. This post has orders, in case of an attack by the enemy, the guns must maintain their fire even after the Infantry have retired.	
	Sept 9th		2 teams of "B" section and 2 of "C" section relieved. 4 teams of "D" section at FERDINAND FARM. 4,000 rounds expended in night firing.	
	Sept 10th		2 teams of "B" section relieved about 6 A.M. by two teams of "A" section. 4000 rounds fired in night firing. Three guns fired the brate put up in searchlights and early thinking it the shape was coming from planes. This only happened when the 2 night guns fired. These were engaging the LEKKERBOTERBEEK Stream. Work commenced on barrage emplacements at HAANIXBEEK. Emplacements to be dug here for 16 barrage guns.	

WAR DIARY or INTELLIGENCE SUMMARY

Army Form C. 2118.

Place: **Wab referens POELCAPELLE 10000 Edition 2**

Date	Hour	Summary of Events and Information	Remarks and references to Appendices
Sep 11th		The four guns at FERDINAND FARM to act as anti-Aircraft guns in addition to their ordinary duties. The A.A. guns at MURAT CAMP unsuccessfully engaged a flight of 4 E.A. at 11 A.M. 4000 rounds fired on enemy trenches etc. and in co-operation with the Heavies. Aeroplane on ROSE COTTAGE, hoping to "pick off" Salvage parties after the H.A. had ceased.	APM a 2nd
Sep 12th		Four guns at FERDINAND FARM relieved by 2 guns of "D" and 2 of "C" sect. n. Guns at HANNIBEEK relieved by two guns of "A" section. 4 E.A's engaged by 2 guns on A.A. duty at MURAT CAMP. The S.A.A. dump made on the MILITARY ROAD, W. of STEEN BEEK. 10,000 rounds dumped here in all. 3 different dumps made. 3,500 rounds fired on trenches. 2 E.A. engaged.	
Sep 13th		2 guns on A.A. duties at MURAT CAMP engaged 1 E.A. flying low. 1 E.A. flying low. E.A. retired in easterly direction. 8750 rounds fired in barrage between 4 P.M. and midnight, and 150 rounds on E.A. by FERDINAND FARM guns. 60,000 rounds placed in dump at FERDINAND FARM, and carrying to HANNIBEEK commenced.	
Sep 14th		Guns at HANNIBEEK relieved by 2 teams of "D" section. Guns at FERDINAND FARM carried out night firing and also co-operated with artillery shoots. 2 E.A. engaged. 0. lot of work done at HANNIBEEK has been blotted out by the enemy. Two new emplacements have nearly disappeared. 35000 rounds S.A.A. carried to HANNIBEEK and dumped at V.29.d.45-05 V.29.d.15.10.	
Sep 15th		Guns at FERDINAND FARM relieved by four guns of "A" section and two of "B" section. 8000 rounds fired during Chinese barrage. 2000 rounds fired indirect on WHITE HOUSE and PHEASANT FARM. Between 10 and 11 P.M. 3000 rounds was fired in a barrage scheme. 100 rounds expended on low flying E.A. SAA carrying proceeded with.	

Army Form C. 2118.

WAR DIARY
INTELLIGENCE SUMMARY.
(Erase heading not required.)

No. 232 COY. M.G.C.

Place	Date 1917	Hour	Summary of Events and Information	Remarks and references to Appendices
War reserve Poelcappelle Ed. 2.	Sep 16th		Guns at HAANIXBEEK relieved by two teams of "B" Section. Work on emplacements and dumps proceeded with. Night firing 4000 rounds 200 at E.A.	Appx 1 & 2.
	Sep 17th		Forward barrage position reconnoitred. 4 guns cooperated with Artillery Shoots 3500 rounds fired indirect on hostile Work on emplacements proceeded with.	
	Sep 18th		Relief of FERDIN AND FARM by two teams of "A" and two teams of "C" Section. Relief of HAANIXBEEK by two teams "C" Section. X day. 10 barrage guns, all belt boxes and firm kit sent up to position, and Lt Henderson ordered to move to forward position. Lt Woolhead arrived to lay 12 guns at HAANIXBEEK at dawn Y day (19th). Guns liberated at 9.45 p.m. Casualties No 71652 Mason. T Shrapnel wounded.	
	Sep 19th		Y day. H.A. Bombardment commenced at 3.30 A.M. Fired orders for barrage batteries issued.	
	Sep 20th		The Division attacked at 5.40 A.M. with the 20th Division on the left and the 55th Division on the right. The first objective being the LANGEMARCK - CHEVOLT line from WHITE HOUSE on the left to VIEILLES MAISONS on the right. By 12 midnight on the night 19/20 the 16 guns of the Company were in positions as follows:- 4 guns in Shell hole emplacements grouped round a Concrete blockhouse by the end the LANGEMARCK WINNIPEG road at about V2g.d.7.3 (known as "S" Battery. 12 guns in shell hole emplacements grouped round the concrete blockhouse known as HAANIXBEEK FARM C5b.3.6 (known as "R" Battery and "S" Battery. 16 belt boxes per gun were nearly filled and there were 30,000 rounds at "S" Battery and 120,000 rounds at HAANIXBEEK in bulk.	

WAR DIARY / INTELLIGENCE SUMMARY

Place: POELCAPELLE
Date: 1917 Sep 20

The laying of all guns was checked at dusk on the 19th, one man of gun being at the position on the 19th for the purpose. The remaining personnel joining after dusk on the night 19/20. The communication were arranged as follows –

Company Head quarters were established at FERDINAND FARM, and telephonic communication laid from here to H.Q. 3 Officers at HAANIXBEEK, who were in turn connected to the Officer at "S2" position, who were connected with Advanced Batty. Headquarters at SNIPE HOUSE. In nearly the whole was cut by intermittent shelling before zero, in several places, and though many attempts were made to repair it, all communication fell upon Runners.

As the control of fire for 12 guns at HAANIXBEEK was clearly very difficult, the following method was employed and found very valuable in the Office. Lt Pulley, with two watches, placed himself in a position from where all the Gun Controllers could see him, and by means of an alternate Red and White light, signalled Fire and "Cease Fire", while a Special Signal was arranged to the guns to lift.

At 5.40 Zero hour all the guns opened fire simultaneously with the Artillery intense barrage and continued at the rate of 3,750 rounds a hour until 6 am when all guns lifted to support the Infantry advance at the Blue line.

The enemy put a strong barrage down between the two groups of Guns from about the LANGEMARCK Road, and within 10 minutes of Zero, Lt Holmes commanding "R1" Battery was wounded, his place being immediately taken by his Sergeant, and the rate of fire kept up. At "R2" Battery, Lieut Webb's Sergeant, who was assisting him in the control and checking of the guns, was also hit,

WAR DIARY
INTELLIGENCE SUMMARY

(Erase heading not required.)

Map reference POELCAPELLE Edn. 2

Place	Date	Hour	Summary of Events and Information	Remarks and references to Appendices
	1917 Sep 20		A section Lance Corporal replacing him. Fire was continued on this line, at a varying rate until 7.29 AM, when all guns lifted on to the S.O.S., and continued firing on this while the protective Artillery barrage lasted, when fire slackened down to intermittent, while belts were changed, emplacements mended, water jackets filled &c., for each gun in turn. During all this time the hostile shelling was fairly continuous, and the gun numbers were shaky in only having 1 O.R. wounded and 1 Lance Corporal killed, though men and guns were covered with dirt from the shells, and several of the emplacements were damaged. During these 3 hours it is calculated that about 102,000 rounds were fired, and all guns, bar one, were in action though in several cases minor breakages occurred. The one gun referred to above had a broken connecting rod at about Zero plus one hour. Orders were then issued for a intermittent fire to be kept up until dusk when all guns were to stop, then the barrage to steady firing again. During the late morning however, Brigade reported a concentration of enemy in various places. As the S.O.S. line had been divided into sectors, it was an easy matter in each case to concentrate the fire of all 15 guns on the threatened quarter, and each place in turn was dealt with either intense or steady fire. From 5.30 pm onwards, numerous of the wounded as they passed the gun positions & Company HQrs. reported that the enemy were attacked on its left flank in great strength, and that the line also was yielding before them. At about 6 pm several wounded Machine gunners of the 154th M.G. Coy. arrived, including a reliable Corporal, who stated that the Infantry had retired, and in consequence their guns had also lost, and stating that the Germans were almost in the RAT HOUSE line. As the position seemed serious, the Company Commander decided to form a defensive flank with the 12	

WAR DIARY
INTELLIGENCE SUMMARY

Place	Date	Hour	Summary of Events and Information	Remarks and references to Appendices
POELCAPELLE	1917 20th Sep		HAANIXBEEK Guns. As, in their barrage positions they were almost useless for defensive work, while the 4 "S2" guns, who were already in a fwd defensive position remained where they were. The Guns were therefore moved, and a defensive flank formed with guns at 25 yards intervals, from in front of the HAANIXBEEK FARM to about C5a 5.5., the spare numbers being established as Infantry, with fixed bayonets, in shell holes between the guns; all guns being laid on the near crest in front of RAT HOUSE. The Captain Commander then reported to the Brigade by 'phone from Advanced Bde. H. Qrs., and was informed that the Counter attack had broken down, and that the enemy was once more retiring rapidly. In consequence Brigade ordered all guns once more on the S.O.S. line, to form a barrage for the retreating enemy to pass through. By about 7.30 pm guns were once more in their barrage positions, and fire was again opened on the S.O.S. line. Casualties during the Counter-Attack. 2. O.R. wounded. The remainder of the night passed fairly quietly, the guns firing intermittently on their S.O.S. line.	
	Sep 21st		The 21st passed fairly quietly, until evening, when S.O.S. went up all along the line, all guns firing until normal condition. On the night 21/22, eight guns were withdrawn to MURAT CAMP, leaving 4 guns at HAANIXBEEK FARM, and 4 near SNIPE HOUSE. The total number of rounds expended during 24 hours was about 162,000.	

Map reference POELCAPELLE 1/10,000 Ed. 2.

WAR DIARY
or
INTELLIGENCE SUMMARY
(Erase heading not required.)

Army Form C. 2118.

No. 232 COY. M.G.C.

Place	Date	Hour	Summary of Events and Information	Remarks and references to Appendices
Map reference. PUELCAPELLE	1917 Sep 22		Guns fired 3,500 rounds during the night, in harassing the enemy's Communications. Both battery positions being subjected to heavy intermittent Shell fire throughout the 24 hours.	
	Sep 23		Gun positions shelled intermittently throughout the day. At dusk the enemy attempted a Counter-attack on the Divisional front, Guns firing a barrage on the S.O.S. line. The attack was beaten off with ease. During the remainder of the night, Cuts were made, and any places there movements were suspected, were intermittently fired on, 4,000 rounds being expended. At 2.A.M. the personnel of the SNIPE HOUSE guns was relieved.	
Map reference: BELGIUM. Sheet 28.	Sep 24th		Gun position shelled intermittently during the day. Harassing fire carried out until 10 P.M. When the Division being relieved, the Guns withdrew to SIEGE CAMP.	
Map reference HAZEBROUCK. 5B & LENS. 11.	Sep 26		Advance party proceeded to VI Corps area.	
	Sep 30th		The Company entrained at HOPOUTRE STN. at 4.40 P.M. and proceeded by train to VI Corps Rest area, detraining at BAPAUME (MAIN STN) at 11 P.M.	
	Oct 1st		Camp at ACHIET LE PETITE reached at 4 A.M.	

Vol 4

Confidential
War Diary
of
232nd Co. Machine Gun Corps.

From 1st to 31st October, 1917

Army Form C. 2118.

No. 21 (A)
HIGHLAND DIVISION

WAR DIARY
INTELLIGENCE SUMMARY.
(Erase heading not required.)

Place	Date 1917	Hour	Summary of Events and Information	Remarks and references to Appendices
Map reference 51.b M.16.c.90.40. Map reference France 51.B.S.W.	Oct 4th		Eight guns with teams proceeded from ACHIET. LE. PETITE, to CARLISLE. CAMP. At 9.30 p.m. 4 guns relieved 245 M.G. Coy. at positions 59.A and 61.n (Map reference left sector 51.b. 0.13.d. 20.80. and 0.13.f. 15.95.) and 4 guns relieved at positions 50.A, 51.A, 52.A, and 53.A. (Map reference 51.b. N.36.a. 30.60. N.30.d. 30.80. N.36.f. 80.50. 0.19.c. 30.10) right sector.	Conference re dug-outs to be improved.
"	Oct 5th		Remainder of Company Came ACHIET. 6.15 a.m. and proceed to CARLISLE CAMP, arriving there at 11.15 a.m, with the exception of "C" Section, (Lieuts Woodhead and O'Leary and 35 O.R's) who proceeded to ARRAS, having now been struck off Company strength. Section transport and 1 Officers charger accompanies them	
"	Oct 6th		Lieut. A.J. Stewart left to take command of a Company.	
"	Oct 7th		Night firing carried out in accordance with instructions.	
"	Oct 8th	7 p.m.	"B" Section relieved "A" in right sector at 7 p.m.	

WAR DIARY

INTELLIGENCE SUMMARY

Army Form C. 2118.

Place	Date 1917	Hour	Summary of Events and Information	Remarks and references to Appendices
Map reference France 51B.S.W.	Oct 9		Night firing as per instructions	
	Oct 10		Night firing as per instructions	
	Oct 11.		2 Guns in Right sector brought out of line, leaving remaining 2 in EGRET TRENCH and EGRET LOOP. Night firing carried out as per instructions	
	Oct 12.		Night firing carried out as per instructions	
	Oct 13.	7 AM	"A" section relieved "D" section in Left sector, RAKE TRENCH. Headquarters in Right sector removed from N.30.d.40.60 to N.30.b.55.45. Night firing carried out as per instructions	Conference, Emplacements, inspected
	Oct 14.		2 Guns in Left sector ("A" section) carried out protective fire, in a raid by Division on Left, according to instructions. 7000 rounds expended.	
	Oct 15		Night firing carried out as per instructions	
	Oct 16.	6.30 pm	Relief. Officer and 2 teams of "B" section, relieved Officer and two teams of "B" in Right sector	

WAR DIARY
INTELLIGENCE SUMMARY

(Erase heading not required.)

Army Form C. 2118.

Place	Date	Hour	Summary of Events and Information	Remarks and references to Appendices
Map reference France 51.B.S.W.	1917 Oct 27		2 teams of "B" section relieved 2 teams of "B" in right sector. Night firing carried out as per instructions.	Subsequently chapters referenced
	Oct 28th	6 p.m.	2/Lt Broadbent relieved Lt Pailey in left sector. 4 teams of "D" section relieved 4 teams of "A".	
		6:30 p.m.	2/Lt Parker relieved Lt Webb in right sector. Night firing carried out.	
	Oct 29		Night firing carried out.	
	Oct 30		Night firing as per instructions.	
	Oct 31	6 p.m.	All guns relieved by 240th M.G. Coy 34th Division. Remainder of Company left CARLISLE CAMP, 12 noon, and marched to rest billets at MONTENESCOURT, arriving 3 p.m. & 4 p.m.	

D Wimberley Capta
Commanding
232 M.G.Coy

WAR DIARY
or
INTELLIGENCE SUMMARY.

(Erase heading not required.)

Army Form C. 2118.

Instructions regarding War Diaries and Intelligence Summaries are contained in F. S. Regs., Part II. and the Staff Manual respectively. Title pages will be prepared in manuscript.

Place	Date	Hour	Summary of Events and Information	Remarks and references to Appendices
Map reference France 51.B.S.W.	1917 Oct 17th		Night firing carried out as per instructions.	Employments, dug-outs &c. inspected
"	Oct 18th		Night firing carried out as per instructions. 2/Lt Henderson and 4 teams of "D" section	
"	Oct 19th	6.30pm	relieved 2/Lt Pulley and 4 teams of "A" section in left sector.	
		10am	2/Lt Barker takes the place of 2/Lt Dixon (sick) in right sector. Night firing	
"	Oct 20th		Night firing carried out in accordance with instructions.	
"	Oct 21st		Night firing as per instructions.	
"	Oct 22nd	6.30pm	2 teams of "B" section relieved 2 teams of "B" in right sector.	
			Night firing carried out as per instructions.	
"	Oct 23rd	6pm	2/Lt Webb relieved 2/Lt Barker in right sector.	
			Night firing carried out as per instructions.	
"	Oct 24th		Night firing carried out as per instructions.	
"	Oct 25th	4pm	2/Lt Pulley relieved 2/Lt Henderson in left sector.	
			Night firing carried out.	
"	Oct 26		Night firing carried out as per instructions.	

Sgt 5

Confidential

War Diary

of

232nd Co. M.G. Corps.

From 1st to 30th November, 1917

232 h.L.C.

WAR DIARY
of
INTELLIGENCE SUMMARY

CONFIDENTIAL
No 1114
ORDERLY ROOM
No 232 COY. M.G.C.
HIGHLAND DIVISION

Army Form C. 2118.

Place	Date 1917	Hour	Summary of Events and Information	Remarks and references to Appendices
Map ref. LENS 11. Edition 2 1/100.000. France 57c SE	Nov 1st to Nov 14th inclusive		Training and rest at MONTENESCOURT.	
	Nov 15		2/Lt Henderson proceeded YTRES to lay S.A.A. dump at BEAUCAMP.	
	Nov 16	6 p.m.	Transport left MONTENESCOURT for COURCELLES arriving there 1 am 17th inst.	
	Nov 17th	8 am	Company entrained at BEAUMETZ, detrained BAPAUME 12 noon, Marched to ROCQUIGNY arriving there 3 p.m. Transport left COURCELLES, 6.45 p.m. arriving at ROCQUIGNY. 2 am 18th inst.	
	Nov 18th	4.45 pm	Company left ROCQUIGNY and marched to METZ, arriving there 8.30 p.m. Transport left at 5.30 p.m. arriving at Transport lines NEUVILLE 10 p.m. Echelon B men stayed with Transport	
	Nov 19th		Final preparations for the line. Officers reconnoitred positions during the day	

Army Form C. 2118.

WAR DIARY
INTELLIGENCE SUMMARY

Place	Date 1917	Hour	Summary of Events and Information	Remarks and references to Appendices
Map reference France 57C S.E.	Nov 20	1.30am	Company marched off and took up positions in line. (SHAFTESBURY AVENUE TRENCH, H.Qrs., dug-out 57C S.E. Q11c) by 4.A.m.	
		6.20am	Attack launched	
		6.55am	12 guns of A.B.D. sections advanced to pre-arranged position in German front line, and barrage line in front of FLESQUIERES. Pack animals (10) supplied ammunition to this position and later on to the forward position. 30,000 rounds expended. Guns were then taken forward to positions in Unseen Trench.	
MARCOING. 57C N.E.	Nov 21	3.30pm	4 gun barrage BEETROOT FACTORY line 6.15am to 6.45am (Company Squad, H.Qrs.) and first transport moved to FLESQUIERES.	
	Nov 22	9pm	2/Lt Brockhead with "D" section and 4 guns proceeded to CANTAING.MILL. and took up positions for Divisional left flank defence.	
	Nov 23	1.31am	2/Lt Henderson with "A" section (4guns) proceeded to CANTAING. to follow up our attack and eventually to take up positions on right of FONTAINE, for defence of right flank.	

WAR DIARY
or
INTELLIGENCE SUMMARY.

Army Form C. 2118.

(Erase heading not required.)

No. 232 Coy. M.G.C.

Place	Date 1917	Hour	Summary of Events and Information	Remarks and references to Appendices
Buire Bapaume	Nov 26	3 am.	All guns relieved and brought back to FLESQUIERES.	
		12 noon	Company marched off from FLESQUIERES to YTRES, arriving there 6 p.m.	
	Nov 27th	11 am.	Company entrained at YTRES and arrived at AVELUY 2.40 p.m. Marched to FUSILIER HUTS, arriving there 3.30 p.m. Transport travelled by road, arriving FUSILIER HUTS at 4.15 p.m.	
LENS. 11.	Nov 28th to Nov 29th		Rest and training at FUSILIER HUTS, BOUZINCOURT.	
	Nov 30th	2.15 p.m.	Received orders to prepare to move to BARASTRE via BAPAUME. Transport proceeded by road to BARASTRE, arriving there 1.30 a.m. 1.12.17. Company entrained at ALBERT, 8.30 p.m., arriving BARASTRE CAMP 2.40 a.m. 1.12.17.	

Capt P Lt
for O.C.
232 M.G.C.

Vol. 6

Confidential
War Diary
of
232nd Co. M.G. Corps
From 1st to 31st December, 1917

Army Form C. 2118.

WAR DIARY
or
INTELLIGENCE SUMMARY.
(Erase heading not required.)

Instructions regarding War Diaries and Intelligence Summaries are contained in F. S. Regs., Part II. and the Staff Manual respectively. Title pages will be prepared in manuscript.

Place	Date	Hour	Summary of Events and Information	Remarks and references to Appendices
Map reference				
	1.12.17		Company at BARASTRE. Capt. Winterley takes over duties of D.M.G.O. Orders received to move, on the morrow, to FRÉMICOURT.	
LENS. II.	2.12.17	9am	Company moves off by march route to FRÉMICOURT (I26.c.6.2.) arriving here at 10.15 am.	
		11am	Received orders for 12 guns to relieve No. 193 and 167 Companies in the line	
FRANCE 57 C N.E.		9pm	Relief complete. 8 guns at D.29.a.10.50 and 4 guns at J.3.c.6.5, J.4.c.8.7, and 9.6, and J.10.b.10.70. Headquarters of Company, Sunken Road, J.2.c.7.7.	
	3.12.17		Situation normal	
	4.12.17	4pm	2/Lt. Broadbent relieved Lt. Webb at rear positions J.3.d.6.5 etc.,	
		10.30pm	2 guns of forward guns relieved by 152 Coy; and other 6 guns withdrawn.	
	5.12.17		Situation normal.	
	6.12.17		Gun positions reconnoitred on BEAUMETZ – MORCHIES line. 3 guns ready to take up positions on this line at 1 hours notice	
	7.12.17	3pm	Teams of "D" section relieved teams of "B" in reserve line. The guns in these positions lay down a barrage on no mans land on S.O.S. signal, night firing impracticable	
	8.12.17		During night of 8-9th positions at J.4.c.80.70, and 90.60, were shelled with 5.9s, and gas shells. Wall near positions hit. Gaps camouflaged later, to prevent enemy viewing village, LOUVERVAL.	

WAR DIARY
or
INTELLIGENCE SUMMARY.
(Erase heading not required.)

Army Form C. 2118.

Place	Date	Hour	Summary of Events and Information	Remarks and references to Appendices
	9.12.17	2pm	2/Lt Broadbent relieved by 2/Lt Mors at T.10.d. 10.70.	
	10.12.17		A further gun put in the line at position "S2" T.11.a.7.7.	
	11.12.17		S.O.S. lines and defensive lines altered and aiming sticks laid out.	
	12.12.17	3pm	Teams of "A" section relieve teams of "D" section.	
	13.12.17	3pm	2/Lt Mors relieved by Lt. Pulley.	
	14.12.17		Alterations to emplacements arranged, and work started.	
	15.12.17		Order boards completed for each emplacement. The 5 emplacements now known as S2, R6, R7, R8, R9.	
	16.12.17		Wiring required in front of positions R7 and R8. Work started.	
	17.12.17		Positions R7 and R8, and S2, shelled early morning with 5.9's.	
	18.12.17	3pm	Lt Pulley and teams of "A" section relieved by 2/Lt Barker and teams of "B" section.	
	19.12.17		Work on emplacements continued, also wiring. Alterations in S.O.S. lines made and Order boards and aiming sticks corrected accordingly.	
	20.12.17		Situation normal. The 5 guns now at emplacements, S2, R5, R6, R7, R8.	
	21.12.17		Situation normal. Work continued.	
	22.12.17		Situation normal.	

WAR DIARY
or
INTELLIGENCE SUMMARY.
(Erase heading not required.)

Army Form C. 2118.

Place	Date	Hour	Summary of Events and Information	Remarks and references to Appendices
	23.12.17		Situation normal. 2/Lt Broadbent and teams of "D" Section relieve 2/Lt Barton and teams of "B" Section	
	24.12.17		Situation normal. Work continued.	
	25.12.17		Situation normal	
DEMICOURT K7c 9.4.	26.12.17	6pm	4 additional guns relieve 242 Coy. in right sector (57°M.E. K7 c 9.3.) Relief completed by Lt. Webb and teams of "B" Section	
	27.12.17		Situation normal. Parties of enemy seen behind their lines in Right Sector	
	28.12.17		2/Lt Moss and teams of "A" Section relieved by 2/Lt. Broadbent and teams of "D" Section in Left Sector. Work on emplacements complete.	
DEMICOURT K2 & 90.95	29.12.17		Situation normal. Enemy party seen near Water Tower, Right Sector.	
	30.12.17	10am	New Section (C) arrived. Situation normal.	
	31.12.17	5pm	2/Lt Henderson and 4 teams relieved Lt. Webb and 4 teams in Right Sector	

— Confidential —

Vol 7

War Diary

of

232nd Co. M.G. Corps.

From 1st to 31st Jan., 1918.

WAR DIARY
INTELLIGENCE SUMMARY
(Erase heading not required.)

Army Form C. 2118.

Instructions regarding War Diaries and Intelligence Summaries are contained in F. S. Regs., Part II. and the Staff Manual respectively. Title pages will be prepared in manuscript.

Place	Date	Hour	Summary of Events and Information	Remarks and references to Appendices
DEMICOURT K.7.c.9.4 and 57 S N E FRANCE	1919 Jan 1st		Situation normal.	
"	" 2		R5 position in left sector badly shelled. One casualty, and position evacuated.	
"	"	4pm	2/Lt. McFarlane relieved 2/Lt. Moss in left sector.	
"	Jan 3rd	9am	R5 position again badly shelled. The gun moved from this position to position at J.10.a.50.80. S2 position is now known as S7.	
"	Jan 4		Situation normal.	
"	Jan 5		Lt. Robillard (C Section) relieved 2/Lt. Henderson in right sector. Lewis also relieves.	
"	Jan 6		Company Commander, Capt. D. Winterbottom, reports the Company from leave and took over command from Lieut. C.H. Hastings.	
"	Jan 7		Gun teams of five guns in left sector relieved by "B" Section.	
"	Jan 8		Situation normal.	
"	Jan 9		Lt. Palley and four guns of "A" section relieved four guns of "C" Section in right sector.	

WAR DIARY
INTELLIGENCE SUMMARY.
(Erase heading not required.)

Army Form C. 2118.

No. 232 COY. M.G.C.

Place	Date	Hour	Summary of Events and Information	Remarks and references to Appendices
DEMICOURT KT 9.4 57 C N E FRANCE.	1918 Jan 10		The Division on the right reported a concentration of enemy's troops on their front, groups of men being seen advancing over the open throughout the morning. An order was received by 2 p.m. from Division to place two guns to defend the right flank of the Divisional front. Two guns were placed in Rows Walsh Support Trench to fulfill the task, being in position by 6pm. Position on CAMBRAI ROAD. S. OF LOUVERVAL shelled continuously during the day. No damage done to deep dug-out.	
			During the early morning two open emplacements constructed for rear gun positions in WALSH SUPPORT.	
	Jan 12		Situation normal.	
	" 13		Situation normal.	
	" 14		Situation normal.	
	" 15		During the morning two guns in INNISKILLING TRENCH and two guns in WALSH SUPPORT relieved by four guns of 154. M.G. Coy. The four guns relieved by 154 Coy then relieved four guns of 152 M.G. Coy in Intermediate Line in the vicinity of DOIGNIES.	

Army Form C. 2118.

WAR DIARY
or
INTELLIGENCE SUMMARY.
(Erase heading not required.)

Place	Date	Hour	Summary of Events and Information	Remarks and references to Appendices
DEMICOURT K7c.9.4 and FRANCE 57c	1918 Jan 16		Situation normal.	
"	Jan 17		Situation normal.	
"	" 18		Company Commander took O.C. relieving Company round the line preparatory to handing over. Slightly increased artillery activity.	
"	Jan 19		11 guns in line relieved during the evening by 11 guns of the 192nd M.G. Coy. Enemy unusually active all day and relief hampered by shell-fire. Relief complete by 8.30 p.m., 1 O.R. being wounded.	
"	Jan 20		Company moved off at 11.30 am to rest billets. Transport at 10.30 am, Arriving COURCELLES-LE-COMPTE No 1 Camp at 2 p.m. and 3 p.m. Company joined 153rd Infantry Brigade Group.	
	Jan 21		Cleaning up and Inspection. Training commenced.	
	Jan 22			
	Jan 23 to Jan 31st		Training and Rest at COURCELLES.	

D Wateleye
O.C.
232 M.G. Coy.

W☩8

Confidential
War Diary
of
232nd Co. M.G. Corps.
From 1st to 28th February 1918.

Army Form C. 2118.

WAR DIARY
INTELLIGENCE SUMMARY.
(Erase heading not required.)

ORDERLY ROOM
No. ....
Date ...4../.3./18.
No. 232 COY. M.G.C.

Place	Date 1918	Hour	Summary of Events and Information	Remarks and references to Appendices
COURCELLES (2000)	Feb 1st to Feb 6th		Training and rest at COURCELLES	
"	Feb 7th		Field Day. Two half sections employed in attack on COURCELLES	
"	Feb 8th		Company and Transport inspected by G.O.C.	
"	Feb 9th		Demonstration of M.G. fire by two half sections for G.O.C.	
FRANCE 57c N.W.	Feb 10th		Company leave Camp at COURCELLES. Personnel entrain at ACHIET and detrain LEBUCQUIRE and occupy huts in SHACKLETON CAMP. Transport travel by road.	
"			12 guns relieve 192 M.G. Coy. in the line :—	
"			4 in Support line	
"			4 at LOUVERVAL.	
"			4 in BEAUMETZ – MORCHIES line.	
FRANCE Part of 57c	Feb 11th		Remainder of Company and Transport move to Camp at FREMICOURT.	
FRANCE 57c N.W.	Feb 12th		Company Headquarters with Transport and remaining personnel remove to COKE CAMP.	
"			LEBUCQUIERE Remaining section, 4 guns, are in reserve here, under orders to move forward at short notice, in case of hostile attack.	

WAR DIARY
INTELLIGENCE SUMMARY.
(Erase heading not required.)

Army Form C. 2118.

No. 232 COY. M.G.C.

Instructions regarding War Diaries and Intelligence Summaries are contained in F. S. Regs., Part II. and the Staff Manual respectively. Title pages will be prepared in manuscript.

Place	Date 1918	Hour	Summary of Events and Information	Remarks and references to Appendices
FRANCE part of 57c.	Feb 13th		Situation normal. Night firing carried out from Support Line.	
"	Feb 14		Situation normal. Night firing carried out as per instructions.	
"	Feb 15		Capt. Winterby takes over duties of A.D.M.G.O. Lieut Hastings takes over temporary command of the Company.	
"		7pm	Lieut Webb and teams of "B" section relieve 2/Lt Broadbent and teams of "D" section in Support Line.	
"		8pm	"D" section in turn relieve "C" in Reserve line LOUVERVAL.	
"		9pm	"C" in turn relieve "A" in BEAUMETZ - MORCHIES line. "A" section returns to Transport Lines	
"	Feb 16.	9.30am	3 enemy aeroplanes were dispersed by rifle fire from No.1 team "B" section in Support Line.	
"	Feb 17.		Improvements to Emplacements &c continuing.	
"	Feb 18		Situation normal.	
"	Feb 19		Reshuffle of the guns in Support Line and intermediate line carried out. Small enemy parties were seen all day on ridge D2VC. These were engaged by rifle fire.	

WAR DIARY

INTELLIGENCE SUMMARY.

(Erase heading not required.)

Army Form C. 2118.

Place	Date	Hour	Summary of Events and Information	Remarks and references to Appendices
FRANCE				
Pont of 57°	Feb 20	6 p.m.	2/Lt Barker and teams of "A" Section took over from Lt. Webb and teams of "B" section in Support Line.	
"	"	7 p.m.	Lt. Webb and teams relieved 2/Lt Broadbent and teams in Intermediate Line.	
"	"	8.30 p.m.	2/Lt Broadbent and teams relieved 2/Lt Mera and teams in BEAUMETZ–MORCHIES Line	
"	"		2/Lt Hoas and teams returned to Transport Lines.	
"	Feb 21	6.20 p.m.	Enemy shelled water point at 710f 10.65. destroying water tank and wounding two men of ration party. Improvements continuing.	
"	Feb 22		Situation normal.	
"	Feb 23		Night firing carried out on E.19.d.	
"	Feb 24		Continuation of work and improvements.	
"	Feb 25	6 p.m.	2/Lt Mamers and teams of "C" Section take over in Support Line	
"	"	7 p.m.	2/Lt Barker and teams take over in Intermediate Line	
"	"	8.15 p.m.	Lt. Webb and teams take over in BEAUMETZ–MORCHIES Line.	
"	"		2/Lt Broadbent and teams return to Transport Lines.	
"	Feb 26		Situation normal.	

WAR DIARY
INTELLIGENCE SUMMARY.
(Erase heading not required.)

Army Form C. 2118.

Place	Date 1918	Hour	Summary of Events and Information	Remarks and references to Appendices
	Feb 27th		Night firing from Support Line	
	Feb 28th		Situation normal.	

Instructions regarding War Diaries and Intelligence Summaries are contained in F. S. Regs., Part II. and the Staff Manual respectively. Title pages will be prepared in manuscript.

www.ingramcontent.com/pod-product-compliance
Lightning Source LLC
Chambersburg PA
CBHW081459160426
43193CB00013B/2536